40

AND

PREGNANT!

DENA KENNEDY

ISBN-10 145284514X
EAN-13 9781452845142

For Jackie Kennedy and Katie Kennedy with all my love. Without you and my wonderful husband, Rick Kennedy, I would not have written this book …

because I would still be clueless!

Thank you for opening my eyes to a whole new world. I will love you forever.

Here is a special quote I found just for you:

Before you were conceived I wanted you
Before you were born I loved you
Before you were here an hour I would die for you
This is the miracle of Mother's Love.
-- Maureen Hawkins

40 AND PREGNANT!

What to expect when you are having your first child at the age of 40

By Dena Kennedy

CONTENTS

i

ACKNOWLEDGMENTS

I would like to thank my biggest supporter, my husband, Rick Kennedy. I would also like to thank my two wonderful daughters, Jackie and Katie, whom I love with every cell in my body. The three of you have made the biggest impact on my life and have taught me so many of life's lessons. Without you, there would be no book. You are everything to me.

I would also like to thank my mother, Jeanie (Sudsbury) Smith. She always wanted a grandchild and made sure I knew that, so I gave her two. Thanks, Mom, for always being there for me and for loving me in spite of myself. Thank you for making the long drive to visit with us, and for not complaining about it. Thank you for letting the girls come and spend a week or more at a time with you so they can truly get to know you. I'm so grateful that the girls have been able to spend that time with you; and I thank God every day that you are alive and healthy and a part of our lives.

Thank you to Rae Richardson, my best friend, who invited me to share her special day – in the labor and delivery room when her daughter Haylee was born. That's a day I'll never forget! (As I'm sure she will never forget the comments I made while there.) Thank you for being the best Vice President that a President could have (back in the days of Bakersfield Legal Secretaries Association). You had my back then, and I knew that you would forever be my friend. Thank you for your love and support over the years. You rock! YBG!

I'd like to thank Wayne and Sherry Smith for always believing in me and supporting me, and never judging me. You are truly amazing and wonderful people. They say you can pick your friends, but you can't pick your family. If I could, you'd be family, as you always will be in my heart. Thank you to Sgt. Ryan Smith, and all Military personnel, for protecting our freedom and serving our Country. And to Kelly Smith-Cameron, the little sister I never had but always wanted.

Thanks to my entire family for love and support, for babysitting, for advice, and for showing my daughters what family is all about.

There are so many people who have made an impression on me and who have helped me along the way. Thanks to each and every one of you.

A special thank you goes out to Ridgely Goldsborough – hey Ridge, I did it!!

**The only thing worth stealing
is a kiss from a sleeping child.**

~Joe Houldsworth

PROLOGUE

Here's the story of how and why I decided to write this book.

It's interesting how you can go through life with no intention or thought of ever writing a book and publishing it, then one day you meet someone and all that changes.

In 2007, I met a man named Ridgely Goldsborough. Ridgely is a columnist, international speaker, and author of The Great Ones. He suggested to me that I write a book. At first, I just laughed it off and said "yeah, right" or something like that. But, he planted the seed. The more I listened to him at motivational and personal development lectures, the more I thought about writing a book.

Ridgely told me to pick a topic that I was passionate about. Then one day it became crystal clear. I would share my experiences as a new and not so young mother so that others could have the resource that I wanted when I was pregnant.

Thank you Ridgely for inspiring me, for believing in me, and for suggesting that I write a book.

Looking back over my notes, I started writing this book on September 9, 2008. At the time, Jackie was 5 years old and Katie was 2 years old. Both my husband and I were working full time jobs. I have no idea how we survived the many sleepless nights. I always thought being a parent would be easy, but that is so far from the truth. Being a mom is the hardest job I've ever held. Maybe that's why some stay at home moms would rather write in "Engineer in the field of Human Development" on the personal information section on forms, rather than "housewife" or "unemployed."

Since everything was a new experience for me, I thought it would be helpful to put it all down in writing. Maybe some day my daughters will read this while they are pregnant.

INTRODUCTION

This book was written for anyone who is over the age of 35 and contemplating having a child, for anyone over the age of 35 who is pregnant, and for anyone who has recently given birth. A woman's body doesn't typically rebound after having children the same way in your late 30's or 40's as it would in your 20's. I will discuss some widely known issues and some issues that most women don't realize . . . until it happens to them. This is not to say don't have a child later in life, but more of a way to relieve the anxiety that a woman feels by not knowing what's in store for her.

I had my first child at the age of 39 and my second child at the age of 42 (it was just 6 weeks before I turned 43). Both of my children were born perfectly healthy and I do not believe my age had any negative consequences for them. At least it didn't at birth . . . who's to say how that may change when they reach sweet 16 and mommy is 55.

This book will address the things that nobody told me about. I didn't know what to expect and was, for the most part, surprised by a lot of things. I hope this book will alleviate some of your fears and make your pregnancy and the years to follow somewhat easier.

I grew up as an only child, so I didn't have the advantage of taking care of younger siblings. So, if you are an only child, or if you are the youngest, this will be particularly helpful to you.

There are pros and cons of having children later in life, because for all of us it's really about whether you see the glass as half full or half empty.

A baby is something you carry inside you for nine months, in your arms for three years and in your heart till the day you die.

-- Mary Mason

CHAPTER 1

AT WHAT AGE SHOULD
YOU HAVE A CHILD?

The right age for one woman is not necessarily the right age for another. Many factors come into play when planning a family. First, I prefer finding the right husband, but maybe I'm just old-fashioned. You should be mature. A child having a child is never a good thing. Grow up first. Live a little. Learn a lot! Finally, you really should be financially secure. Children are not inexpensive.

You either marry a man who can support you and as many children as you want, or you get a good job and work and save your money so that you can afford to take time off when your child is born. Most employers will allow you six weeks off work, with disability pay, for having a baby. Six weeks! Are you kidding me? Okay, you get eight weeks if you have a cesarean section child birth. Seriously? I could barely walk at the four week mark (I had a c-section). Nobody in the house is getting any sleep in greater than two hour increments and you expect me to be a functioning human being and work a regular job after just 8 weeks? Save your money, your sick time and your vacation time so that you can spend at least four to six months with your new baby. You'll be glad you did.

Children are expensive. If you're like me, you're probably thinking to yourself right now "What's one more mouth to feed? It's a small mouth after all." I used to scrunch my face all up when someone would say "I can't afford to have another child" or "my family would be so mad at me if I got pregnant again, I can't afford more children." Huh? How can that be? They're just little people and it's not like your house payment goes up any. It's just a few more groceries, right?

Wrong.

Unless you plan on being a stay-at-home mom who nurses for a full year and washes the baby's cloth diapers, nothing could be further from the truth. Recent studies have estimated the cost for a middle-class family to raise a child (with both parents working) is close to $250,000.00, not including college. Depending on where you live, the cost can be anywhere from $11,000 to $15,000 per year for one child. There may be some breaks for multiple children if the daycare gives a family discount, but don't count on it. Also, if you have two children of the same sex, you can re-use clothes and toys for the second child.

As discussed in another chapter on daycare, being a working mom can mean giving up most of your paycheck just to have someone watch your child(ren). The going rate for infants in a public daycare is around $350 a week.

Formula costs over $30 for a large jar (it's powdered and you mix it with warm water). A large jar will last about two weeks. There's also liquid formula, which is more expensive, but might not have the air bubbles that the power does (when mixed with water and shaken). It all depends on what's best for the baby's digestive tract. Remember, if the baby is happy, the whole family is happy.

Then there are the diapers and wipes. If you have a warehouse store like Costco nearby, you can get case of diapers (usually about 200 in a box) for around $50. The smaller the diaper (the smaller the baby), the more that fit into the box, as most boxes are about the same size and all are the same price. So, if you have an infant in a size 1, you'll get about 260 diapers for $52.00. Whereas a size 6 would still cost the same, but you would only be getting 144 diapers. Funny, at first you spend roughly .20 for a diaper, and as they grow, you are spending .36 per diaper. Figure anywhere from 7 to 12 diapers a day.

Don't forget that each time a diaper is used, so is a wipe . . . and sometimes it's more like 5 wipes – for those really dirty diapers . . . you know what I mean. Wipes from the warehouse cost about $32.00 and you will get 832 wipes. Don't be fooled into thinking that one case of wipes will last as long as four cases of diapers. Babies are fascinated with wipes and as soon as they can move their hands and arms they will begin grabbing the wipes. I've often found my little one in the middle of the living room floor surrounded by wipes that she has pulled out of the box. To them, it's fun. To you, it's money down the drain. You will also use wipes to clean off their hands and face after they eat spaghetti or birthday cake, wiping up spills on the floor, cleaning off the highchair tray, wiping their little noses, etc. They're even good for removing fingerprints off of light switches and on door frames. The list goes on and on. I think I'll go on buying wipes long after my children need them because they're so handy.

So, plan on going thru a minimum of two jars of formula, one case of diapers, one case of wipes every month. Just those three items will cost you $150 a month. Unless you have the firstborn grandchild, you will also need to buy clothes for your new bundle of joy, a stroller, shampoo, powder, diaper rash cream, lotion, shoes, etc. After your child is weaned off formula, there's a time period in which Gerber foods are what's best for your baby and your table scraps are still off limits for the little one. You will need to buy various jars of fruit, vegetables and meat until junior has some teeth and can chew "real" food. These little jars of food are cute, but not necessarily cheap.

When children become fascinated with wipes, they really are quite adorable. Forget about the cost per wipe and just watch their face and the simple amazement as they pull each wipe out, one at a time, and smile at their accomplishment. If you were to look at the world through your baby's eyes, everything would be amazing. They are so easy to please and don't forget that they love you unconditionally, just as you love them. One of the greatest feelings in life is the way a baby looks at you. They show you how they feel long before they can even say "I love you." Their eyes really do twinkle when they are happy. Don't miss out on the little things. Life is all about the little things, the little joys, the seconds of pure happiness. Not everyone gets them, but if you have a new baby in your life, you're sure to get a lot of them.

**Making a decision to have a child--it's momentous.
It is to decide forever to have your heart go
walking around outside your body.**

-- Elizabeth Stone

NOTES:

_____

_____

_____

_____

_____

THINGS TO ASK YOUR DOCTOR:

_____

_____

_____

_____

_____

_____

_____

CHAPTER 2
TWINS

So you're ready to start a family. How many children do you want? If you want two or three, do you want them all at once? If you are over the age of 40, your chance of conceiving twins is much greater than at 20. Whether you are using in vitro fertilization, fertility enhancement medication, or nothing at all, more women in their later years are having twins (or even triplets) than their younger counterparts.

The chance of having twins increases with age; 17% of mothers over the age of 45 give birth to twins. If you want to increase your chances that you will have twins, wait until you are over the age of 45. According to Fun Facts About Multiples, becoming a mother after age 50 boosts your odds considerably, to nearly 1 in 9! These figures are based on population statistics so don't start thinking if you are 50 and you get pregnant 9 times that you are guaranteed twins.

You can increase your odds by taking fertility drugs or undergoing other fertility treatments. Some estimate that the chance of having twins after fertility enhancing treatment is as high as 1 in 38. Others estimate that using the drug Clomid increases your chances to 1 in 5. Again, nothing is guaranteed as each pregnancy is unique.

Aside from fertility drugs, your heredity plays a factor in whether or not you will have twins. If you, your mother, or your grandmother is a fraternal twin, you may carry a gene for hyperovulation, which means you release more than one egg during an ovulation cycle, increasing the ability to conceive fraternal twins. The chances may be high as 1 in 17 if you are a fraternal twin yourself.

If you've already had one set of fraternal twins, your chances of conceiving another set are four times greater than the average woman, or about 1 in 12! However, you must remember that two children are not twice the amount of work as one child. Rather, it seems more like four times the amount of work.

If you're Nigerian, your chance of having twins is estimated at 1 in 22. Some sources attribute it to their consumption of large quantities of yams. Really? Hey, it's worth a try if you really want to have twins (and actually like yams)!

12

Interestingly, if you're overweight or tall, there is a significant increase in fraternal twin births. Mothers who had a BMI of 30 or higher, or who were in the top 25th percentile for height, had a greater chance of having twins according to a study published by the American College of Obstetrics and Gynecology.

Now, if you are over 40 and definitely do not want twins, here are some things that may decrease those odds. If you are Hispanic or Asian, you are substantially less likely to have twins than white or black mothers. Among worldwide populations, the Asian countries of Japan and China have the lowest rates of twins, estimated at 1 in 150 and 1 in 300, respectively. This information is according to a 2001 study by the National Center for Health Statistics.

Geographically speaking, if you live in Hawaii (and I don't mean just moved there when you got married), you are about 30% below the national average for twins.

Ironically, if you want identical twins, the rate for identical, or monozygotic, multiples is random and universal; it's the same in all populations regardless of race, heredity or other factors, and it has remained constant over time. The chance of having identical twins is about 1 in 285.

Then, of course, there is the obvious (which if you're reading this, then it's too late for you). If you are under the age of 25, your chances of having twins is less than half of what it would be after 30.

What? Two is not enough for you? Okay, here's the lowdown on triplets and more. The statistics for higher order multiples have shown that the odds of conceiving spontaneous triplets (without the aid of fertility drugs or procedures) is about 1 in 8,100. Researchers noted a substantial increase of 400% in the rate of triplet births over the last twenty years. The odds of having spontaneous quadruplets are predicted to be 1 in 729,000.

(Note: These statistics are estimates, gathered from several sources, including a 2001 National Vital Statistics Report from the Centers for Disease Control and Prevention, Odds - Twins from BabyMed.com, Facts About Multiples: Twin Basics Page 2 web page, and Twinstuff.com. Also, much of this information was gathered from pages of the website http://multiples.about.com.)

Two faces to wash, and four dirty hands
Two insistent voices, making demands
Twice as much crying, when things go wrong
The four eyes closing, with slumber song
Twice as many garments, blowing on the line
Two cherubs in the wagon, soaking up sunshine
Work I do for twins, naturally comes double
But four arms to hug me, repay all my trouble.

~Author Unknown

NOTES:

_____

_____

_____

_____

_____

_____

THINGS TO ASK YOUR DOCTOR:

_____

_____

_____

_____

_____

_____

_____

CHAPTER 3

MISCARRIAGE

It's true that one of a woman's greatest fears while pregnant is that of having a miscarriage. It's amazing how little this is ever talked about publicly. It is not uncommon (up to 20% of *known* pregnancies end in miscarriage) and doesn't matter what your age is. It also doesn't matter how much you try to do exactly everything the right way. It can still happen. It wasn't until I had one at about the 7 or 8 week mark, that it finally hit me why women wait until they are in the beginning of their second trimester to tell people that they are pregnant. The reason is that most miscarriages

17

happen around the 8 week mark. If there is anything wrong with the egg, zygote, fetus, it will basically self-destruct. This is nature's way of helping out. Of course, I had already told my entire family, my friends and my co-workers that I was pregnant (at about the 2 week mark). After I lost the baby, I had to tell everyone what had happened. Many of you would rather keep the news to yourself until you are certain it's a keeper. It's no fun telling everyone sad news.

The soap operas are notorious for having a pregnant woman fall down a flight of stairs and have a miscarriage, but that doesn't have to be the cause. Your doctor will tell you things to avoid, like picking up heavy objects (your other children, if you have any), and maybe to avoid strenuous exercise the first trimester. However, if it's going to happen, it's going to happen no matter how careful you are.

Some doctors may put you on bed rest, or send you to a specialist for acupuncture or some other form of holistic healing, but you have to remember that it's happening for a reason.

Most obstetricians will not even let you schedule your first pregnancy appointment until you are 8 weeks along. However, in some high risk instances, your doctor may want to see you early and often. Be totally honest with your doctor and remember that they are there to help you.

If you're in store for a miscarriage, you'll know instantly that something is wrong. You'll either start spotting, cramping or having fluid and/or tissue passing from your vagina. Your doctor will likely send you to a lab for some blood tests. They can tell by the level of pregnancy hormone in your blood whether or not you're about to have a miscarriage. I was tested one day and then told to return a day or two later for another test. The pregnancy hormone level had dropped and my doctor knew that I was having a miscarriage. There was nothing I could do to stop it. I did actually slide down the stairs in our house but I'll never know if that was the cause or not. I was standing at the top of the stairs talking to my 2 year old and I twisted so that I was facing the stairs and all of a sudden my feet flew out from under me and I landed on my bottom. Bump, bump, bump down about 10 stairs I went before I could stop myself. I wasn't hurt, but that week is when I had the miscarriage.

Medical reports suggest that women over the age of 35 have a higher risk of miscarriage than do younger women. At 35, it's about a 20 percent risk; at 40, it's about 40 percent; and at 45, it's about 80 percent. The father's age also may play a role. Some studies indicate that the chance of a miscarriage is higher if the father of the baby is 35 or older, with the chance increasing as men age. Of course, smoking and drinking during pregnancy can increase these risk factors.

If you do have a miscarriage, there's no reason to believe that's the end of your child-bearing years. You may try to get pregnant again at your next menstrual cycle (which could come in as little as four to six weeks) or, if you need more time emotionally, wait a little longer. If you have two or three miscarriages in a row, you may want to talk to your doctor about further testing to find out what the cause may be.

I'm not supposed to love you, I'm not supposed to care, I'm not supposed to live my life wishing you were there. I'm not supposed to wonder where you are or what you do...I'm sorry I can't help myself, I'm in love with you.
-- Author Unknown

NOTES:

_____

_____

_____

_____

_____

_____

THINGS TO ASK YOUR DOCTOR:

_____

_____

_____

_____

_____

_____

CHAPTER 4

PRENATAL VITAMINS

There is a reason expectant mothers are told to take prenatal vitamins. If you are contemplating getting pregnant, or you already are pregnant, you need to take your prenatal vitamins! If you are "trying" to get pregnant, the best reason to start taking prenatal vitamins (even the generic ones at the local drug store) is so the "host" of your new fertilized egg is as healthy as can be. Just think about this: When you bring your new baby home from the hospital, are you going to put him in a dirty bassinet? No, you're not. You are going to want everything to be as clean and germ-free as possible. You need to take that same approach to your womb and your entire body. You and only you will be nourishing your baby for 40 weeks. You will want your body to start out in the best condition possible. If you smoke or drink alcohol, stop before conceiving. You will need to stay away from these things when you're pregnant anyway so you might as well get used to it.

Your body will use up virtually all of the nutrients it gets from the food you eat, and it will never be enough. You need to supplement. The prenatal vitamins are like a multi-vitamin. They contain a good amount of folic acid, which helps to prevent birth defects. They also contain iron, which you will need in order to have the energy to get through the day. Everything in the prenatal vitamins is designed to make your body healthy, so it can nourish your baby.

About half way through my second (full term) pregnancy, I stopped taking my prenatal vitamins for a week or two. Why? I'm not sure, it just slipped my mind. At my monthly doctor's appointment, I told my doctor I was very weak and had no energy. She asked if I was taking my vitamins and when I told her I wasn't – oh boy, was I in trouble! She stressed the importance of taking them DAILY and not missing a single dose. I was so anemic that I had to take extra iron supplements for a couple of weeks. Sure enough, as soon as I was back on track and had my prenatal vitamins in my system, I felt much better and I had the energy I needed to get through the day.

There are many types of prenatal vitamins; some are sold over the counter and others are by prescription only. You may have to try a couple of different kinds to see what works best with your system. Some may make you feel nauseous, while others have no adverse effects at all.

Think of stretch marks as pregnancy service stripes.

-- Joyce Armor

NOTES:

_____

_____

_____

_____

_____

_____

THINGS TO ASK YOUR DOCTOR:

_____

_____

_____

_____

_____

_____

_____

CHAPTER 5

MORNING SICKNESS

Are you wondering if you'll have morning sickness? Well, I have good news and bad news. The good news is if you don't have morning sickness with your first child, you are likely not to have it with a second or third pregnancy. The bad news is there's no way of knowing if you'll have morning sickness with your first child until you are actually pregnant. Another tidbit of good news is that morning sickness usually occurs only during the first trimester. However, for those with acute morning sickness the first trimester may seem to last a very long time. In fact, there is no "rule" that says that on the first day of your second trimester all morning sickness will magically be gone. Twelve weeks is just a rough estimate and the most common.

I had three pregnancies and not a single day of morning sickness. I know of nothing I did differently than anyone else. I've always had what we call a cast iron stomach, meaning that I could eat anything at anytime and feel just fine. Taco Bell for breakfast? Sure, no problemo. Cold pizza, no worries. Vitamins on an empty stomach rarely bothered me. It's just how I've always been.

I have a friend, on the other hand, who had morning sickness with her first child, in her 20's, then she got pregnant again in her mid 30's and said her morning (which was actually all day and night) sickness was even worse! She was so bad that even the smell of food would make her run to the restroom, or grab a nearby trashcan. She was so dehydrated that the doctors had to give her fluids.

It seems as if most women experience some type of morning sickness. For those with a light case of it, keeping saltine crackers on your bedside table can calm your stomach before you get out of bed. It seems to have something to do with standing up. You'll be fine lying down, but when you get out of bed, everything just seems to start churning.

Some theorize that the nausea is associated with certain toxins that the mother ingests while pregnant. These so-called toxins will not harm the mother because she has a strong immune system, but they could be very dangerous to the fetus, so the mother gets nauseous and vomits to rid her body of the toxic substances.

You may also notice that your food likes and dislikes change while you are pregnant. Maybe once you liked garlic, but when you are pregnant, the smell of it is enough to gag you. After the baby is born, you may never go back to enjoying garlic on your foods. It's like a reminder of having morning sickness all over again.

Babies are a link between angels and man.

-- Author Unknown

NOTES:

_____

_____

_____

_____

_____

_____

THINGS TO ASK YOUR DOCTOR:

_____

_____

_____

_____

_____

_____

_____

CHAPTER 6

AMNIOCENTESIS

What is amniocentesis? It is a procedure that your doctor will recommend you have if you are 35 or older. The procedure will most likely be performed around your 16th week of pregnancy. Amniocentesis (also referred to as amniotic fluid test or AFT), is a medical procedure used to diagnose genetic abnormalities of the fetus. Specifically, a small amount of amniotic fluid (less than one ounce) is extracted through a fine needle from the amniotic sac – not from the actual baby itself. An ultrasound is used so the technician can see where the fetus is and where the needle is. This greatly reduces the chance that the needle will pierce the baby. The fluid that is removed contains fetal tissues contained in the amniotic sac surrounding the developing fetus. The fetal DNA is then examined for genetic abnormalities. The puncture wound heals much like when you have blood removed from a vein in your arm, however, the needle is much thinner so it actually heals faster.

Why is this done for women over the age of 35? This test can be performed on any age woman, but modern science feels that the risk of having a baby with genetic abnormalities greatly increases after the age of 35. Specific tests are performed to determine if the fetus has Down syndrome, Trisomy 18, sickle cell disease, cystic fibrosis, muscular dystrophy, spina bifida or other genetic defects. Amniocentesis will not detect all birth defects, but it will rule out a great number of them.

What are the risks? There is a small risk (less than 1%) that an amniocentesis could cause a miscarriage. Also, there could be injury to the baby or mother, infection, or preterm labor. But these complications are extremely rare.

On the up side, it's the perfect and foolproof way to find out the sex of your baby. DNA doesn't lie. Also, you will know and be perfectly at ease for the rest of your pregnancy that your baby doesn't have any of the birth defects that were tested. (The testing is up to you and your doctor.) Since this test is performed at around three to four months – you will have five to six months relatively worry-free. The risks are so small compared to how you will feel for the rest of your pregnancy. The stress is gone, the "unknown" is mostly gone, and the anxiety over boy or girl is completely gone (unless you tell the doctor that you absolutely don't want to know the sex of your baby). You can choose not to look at the ultrasound monitor if you're very strong willed and really don't want to know the sex of your baby. I just *had* to know. You can paint the nursery pink or blue, and even throw out all of the yellow and green if you so desire. You begin a journey and a story for generations to come. You tell your family and friends that it's a girl or a boy and then everyone else knows exactly what to buy for your baby shower. You can pick out your baby's name and start calling him or her by name. Your family will start calling the baby by its name too.

My Aunt Donna was pregnant with her fourth child when she was in her 40's and he was a real kicker. When he kicked, she would refer to him as Thumper Junior, and then we all started calling him TJ for short. This went on during her pregnancy and when TJ was born, she had to come up with a name other than Thumper Junior for her baby boy. Today we all know him as Tyler James, or TJ, but a few of us know his *real* name.

If one feels the need of something grand, something infinite, something that makes one feel aware of God, one need not go far to find it. I think that I see something deeper, more infinite, more eternal than the ocean in the expression of the eyes of a little baby when it wakes in the morning and coos or laughs because it sees the sun shining on its cradle.

-- Vincent van Gogh

NOTES:

_____

_____

_____

_____

_____

_____

THINGS TO ASK YOUR DOCTOR:

_____

_____

_____

_____

_____

_____

_____

CHAPTER 7

CORD BLOOD

What is cord blood? Umbilical cord blood is the blood that remains inside the umbilical cord after childbirth that used to just get thrown in the trash. Research has since proven there are a vast number of things that this blood can be used for. Cord blood is collected from the umbilical cord after it has been detached from the baby, so there is no chance of harm to the baby. It is so important because it contains stem cells which can be used to treat genetic disorders. One of the best things about using your own cord blood is that your body's immune system is not likely to reject the stem cells as it may otherwise with someone else's.

I remember being completely blind-sided when the doctor asked me if I wanted to keep the cord blood with my first child. At the time, storing cord blood was relatively new and free, so I said sure, why not? I later found out that this was a public cord blood bank. When my second baby was born I was given a flyer and this time they wanted me to pay for the storage, which I declined. The private cord blood banks cost around $2,000 for collection and then about $125 a year for storage (in 2007). After seeing all of the positive the research on it, I probably should have saved it. My thinking at the time was that I already had the blood from the first child and that was enough. If you do save it, make sure you remember where it is – in case of emergency.

"Regenerative medicine is the next evolution of medical treatments. . . . This revolutionary technology has the potential to develop therapies for previously untreatable diseases and conditions. Examples of diseases regenerative medicine can cure include diabetes, heart disease, renal failure, osteoporosis, and spinal cord injuries." - National Institutes of Health.

According to Dr. Mehmet Oz, "cord blood can be used to help treat nearly fifty different conditions. In fact, there's a 1-in-2,700 chance that your child will need that blood by age twenty-one and an even greater chance that somebody in the family will be able to use it." With that kind of information, I can't imagine a reason not to keep it.

**Babies are bits of stardust, blown
from the hand of God.
-- Barretto**

NOTES:

_____

_____

_____

_____

_____

_____

THINGS TO ASK YOUR DOCTOR:

_____

_____

_____

_____

_____

_____

_____

CHAPTER 8

POST-PARTUM DEPRESSION

Post-Partum Depression ("PPD") is not what you may think. I often wondered why someone with a perfectly healthy baby would have this illness. I even asked a neighbor of mine who suffered from PPD what was going on, but she could not explain it to me. No one in my immediate family ever experienced it, so I just always thought it was an imagined state of mind formed to gather sympathy or to get out of one's duties.

Wow! Was I ever wrong. My first child was born and I went about my business. Never did a PPD thought cross my mind. Oh sure, I had newly gained weight issues and lack of sleep, but was mostly happy because I had a beautiful baby and a loving husband. I was still under the mistaken belief that depression was just an excuse . . . until it happened to me.

Baby number two was born in a much easier circumstance than was my first born. I say "easier" only because I knew what was going on this time and what to expect. I picked out her birthday and scheduled my c-section. She was healthy, so was I. I had an extra month off for maternity leave and enjoyed bonding with my child. I returned to work as planned and then it hit me. I was so completely blindsided by it that I didn't even realize what was happening. I would walk around the office with thoughts going through my head like "I don't want to be here," "I want to just die and go away," and "I wish I wasn't alive." Then I would argue with myself (in my mind), "you can't do that, you have a wonderful husband and two little girls that need their mommy. Snap out of it woman!"

What was happening to me? I didn't even believe in depression. I called my ob/gyn who in fact confirmed that I was suffering from PPD. I asked her what I was supposed to do. She recommended a couple of prescription drugs that I could take, both of which had undesirable side affects. I said I wanted to think about it and would call her later.

I'm sure you know the saying "everything happens for a reason." Well, a girlfriend of mine invited me to lunch that day who knew nothing of my PPD issues. She was involved in a new company and offered me a sample of their nutritional supplements. She said they would give me more energy and also give me the nutrients that I needed after child birth. How nice of her, I thought. Sure I'll take them, why not? What did I have to lose? I took the sample for three days. Not only did they do what she said but they also completely got rid of my PPD! The supplements are from a company called ViSalus Sciences and they come in a "Vi-Pak" which has four components (multi-vitamin, antioxidant, omegas, and a patented anti-aging & energy formula). The Vi-Pak is full of omega 3's and 6's and after much research I found out that that was what was missing from my diet. Only three days on the supplements and I was back to my old self again.

Did you know that Omega Vitals, or Essential Fatty Acids (EFA), are so-named because they are imperative for optimal health, cognitive function and cardiovascular support? Yeah, me neither. The EFA's are identified as omega-3 EFA (or alpha-linolenic acid) and omega-6 EFA (linoleic acid). A deficiency in either progressively results in poor health. Like other essential nutrients, the human body cannot function without EFA's in the diet. EFA's function as building blocks for the membranes of every cell in the body. They also produce "prostaglandin families," which are hormone-like substances necessary for energy metabolism and cardiovascular and immune health. Brain and nerve tissue consist of over 50% EFA's. Whether or not you've just had a baby, these are really good for you.

What good mothers and fathers instinctively feel like doing for their babies is usually best after all.

-- Benjamin Spock

NOTES:

_____

_____

_____

_____

_____

_____

THINGS TO ASK YOUR DOCTOR:

_____

_____

_____

_____

_____

_____

_____

CHAPTER 9

NURSING aka BREAST FEEDING

I won't get into all of the controversy surrounding nursing your baby in public. There are plenty of others who love to stir that pot. Instead, I'd like to tell you what to expect. While it may be the best thing for your baby and make you feel more connected, it will also make you vividly aware of how sensitive your areola can be. Remember when you first started noticing your breasts growing larger as a young girl? Remember how whenever anything touched your breasts or someone accidentally bumped into you, it hurt like crazy? Get ready for round two sister!

The first time you will nurse your baby is in the hospital when he/she is just a few hours old. There is usually a lactation nurse that will come into your room and show you exactly what to do (in case you didn't attend the classes on nursing while you were pregnant). You will be so excited to bond with your baby and feed the little darling that everything will seem magical. Indeed, it is miraculous. However, after a couple of weeks, the constant "attention" your nipples will be receiving will begin to make them very tender, and then downright sore. Fortunately, there are a few topical creams you can apply that will ease the pain. There's a certain threshold that you must pass and then it's over. Whew! Now you can feed your baby and enjoy the precious time you spend together.

What you likely won't enjoy is when you are least expecting it, you start squirting out milk all over your clothes . . . in public! Yes, it's true what everyone says about hearing someone else's baby cry when you are at the grocery store, the mall, the department store, etc. When you are lactating and you hear any baby cry, your milk just starts flowing. So, you'd better invest in some good breast pads (they're like sanitary napkins, they have tape on one side to stick inside your bra) just in case it happens to you.

You will also notice plenty of milk free flowing when you are taking a shower. Don't worry, this is normal and you don't have to be concerned about wasting it because you will produce enough milk for your baby when your baby is feeding. It's the basic principle of supply and demand.

Another thing I found particularly annoying is that it's almost a requirement to wear a bra to bed. Most of us don't even like wearing them during the day! It seems as if whenever your milk comes in and you are "full," it just starts leaking out. If you are getting up every two hours to feed the baby, this might not happen to you, but if and when the baby starts sleeping for 6 hours at a time, you will either wear a bra at night or wake up in a puddle of milk.

Human breast milk is the healthiest form of milk for babies, provided the mother is healthy and is not taking any drugs. Most doctors will recommend breast feeding your baby for six months to a year. While it's a lot cheaper than formula and better for the baby, you may not have the ability to nurse your baby for that long. You may need to return to work earlier than six months and your place of employment may not have a private room for you to pump the milk out during the day. There are many things that can get in the way of nursing your baby for six months (or longer). Some women have low milk production for one reason or another and need to supplement with formula and once you start doing that, the demand is less, so the supply becomes less. Eventually it just dries up.

There are some medications that can be taken to increase milk production. This is something unique to each woman and will need to be discussed with your physician.

There are three reasons for breast-feeding: the milk is always at the right temperature; it comes in attractive containers; and the cat can't get it.

-- Irena Chalmers

NOTES:

_____

_____

_____

_____

_____

_____

THINGS TO ASK YOUR DOCTOR:

_____

_____

_____

_____

_____

_____

_____

CHAPTER 10

CHANGES TO YOUR BODY

Oh you may think you're different because you're 35 and still fit into your high school cheerleading skirt and that you'll bounce right back after having a baby. Sure, some of you might, but most of you won't. Unless you have the money for a personal trainer, a chef, a nutritionist and a nanny, forget about dressing up as a cheerleader on Halloween anytime soon.

I thought I'd be the one or two percent that would just snap back. I was 39, never wore anything bigger than a size 4. Never weighed an ounce over 110 until I was in my 30's and even then stayed under 125. What a rude awakening! I weighed 154 when I gave birth to my first child and was only able to get back down to 133. Amazingly, when I gave birth to my second child I was right around 154 again, but this time 143 was the number that the scale liked the most. At 25 years of age, I could have probably bounced right back. At 43, it was a whole different story.

If you can, nurse your baby for a year. Most doctors recommend a minimum of 3 to 6 months. For various reasons, I was only able to nurse each one for about 3 months. Nursing causes your uterus to contract back to its normal size – or close to it. Nursing also burns a lot of calories. You'll burn an estimated 500 calories a day just nursing your baby. It's hard work for your body but much easier than getting on the treadmill or stair stepper – especially after a c-section. Eat healthy, drink plenty of water and get regular exercise or you will never fit back into your skinny jeans.

You may also notice that certain areas have shifted just a bit. Your nice little hourglass figure may wind up a pear or an apple, but whatever it is, your baby will love you. My oldest even went so far as to tell me that I'm comfortable to sleep on. Oh, so I'm a pillow now? Wonderful.

Do you like your nice manicured fingernails? Well, they might have to go for awhile. Babies do not like being stuck with sharp fingernails. In fact, if you have fingernails, sometimes your baby will try to bend them backwards while they are squeezing your finger. Experience that a couple of times and you'll fire your manicurist.

NOTES:

_____

_____

_____

_____

_____

_____

THINGS TO ASK YOUR DOCTOR:

_____

_____

_____

_____

_____

_____

_____

CHAPTER 11

SLEEP AND YOUR METABOLISM

For anyone trying to lose weight, there are three main components: diet, exercise and sleep. That's right, sleep. Your sleep patterns greatly affect your metabolism. At 20 years of age, your metabolism is fully revved up and can handle a couple years of patchy sleep. At 40, however, sleep is your best friend – only you never really get to enjoy it if you've recently had children. Other than nursing your baby, which will cause your uterus to contract and help you get back to a flat stomach, there's nothing more important than getting quality sleep.

You wonder how the movie stars bounce back into shape so quickly. It's simple. Someone else gets up with their baby in the middle of the night while they enjoy sound, uninterrupted sleep for 8 hours. Best advice: Get a nanny! You may think you can't afford one, but with the rising cost of daycare, you might as well have someone helping you around the house and getting up in the middle of the night for you. You may need to cut out that daily trip to the coffee shop or a couple nights out on the town with your husband, but it's well worth it if you want your figure back.

Don't be surprised if you used to have trouble getting over 110 pounds soaking wet in your 20's and then find yourself struggling to stay under 140 pounds after a couple children in your 40's. Keeping your calorie intake in check is not difficult, however, having the energy to exercise when you're only getting 3 hours of sleep here and there is nearly impossible.

Interestingly, I just read on Oprah's website Dr. Oz's ultimate checklist to better health. After he explained the first nine steps, which included nutrition, supplementation, exercise, regular doctor checkups, etc., he then said that while steps one through nine are important, if you skip rule number 10, you might as well toss the rest out the window. Do you want to know what number 10 is? By far the most *impossible* thing to do – or at least in my home it was – he said you need seven to eight hours of sleep every night. Ha! I used to get 10 hours a night before children and now the most I can get is five or six before being awakened by a little voice down the hall saying "Mommy, I wake up."

Dr. Oz also said, "If you don't get sleep, you'll crave other things like carbohydrates. Sleep will also generate growth hormone. That's the vitality hormone that makes us nice and bouncy and youthful and vigorous and makes us stay beautiful. The best way of getting growth hormone is to sleep the seven hours we speak of."

People who say they sleep like a baby usually don't have one.

-- Leo J. Burke

If your baby is "beautiful and perfect, never cries or fusses, sleeps on schedule and burps on demand, an angel all the time," you're the grandma."

-- Theresa Bloomingdale

NOTES:

_____

_____

_____

_____

_____

_____

THINGS TO ASK YOUR DOCTOR:

_____

_____

_____

_____

_____

_____

_____

CHAPTER 12
YOUR FEET

You have most likely heard that your feet will swell near the end of your pregnancy due to water retention. They do. However, I believe this is lulling women in to a false hope that their feet will return to their normal size after the birth of their child. I have some friends who had children in their 20's and their feet did not grow. Some said their arches dropped and then came back up again later on. So, you may or may not experience this, but it is always nice to be aware of what could happen, especially if you have a shoe fetish!

Now this may be true for any age mother, but it seems as if it is a lot more expensive to deal with as the years pass. For each child that was born, my feet grew exactly one-half a shoe size. I could still squeeze into some of my pricey pumps after my first daughter was born, but by the time the second arrived and I was almost 43, most of my shoes had to go. At 43, I had quite a collection – over 100 pair of dress shoes, casual shoes, tennis shoes, boots, flip flops, slippers. You name it, and I probably had it in many colors. Of course, part of this was because I had nobody to buy for except myself. I loved to shop. I had the latest styles, colors and fashions. I could buy a new pair of shoes every week if I wanted to. Oh, and let's not forget the matching purse collection. I am a business woman and so I had suits in many colors with matching purses and shoes. I still have the purses, although they all reside at the top of my closet since they are almost all too small to put in a few diapers and wipes. Lately, it seems as if everything I own matches with black . . . . including the diaper bag. It's amazing how much you can coordinate with just a few pairs of black shoes.

After interviewing several women, I noticed a pattern that most of the women who were tall, had little change to their feet or shoe size, while shorter women noticed the biggest change to their shoe size. If you think about it, it does make sense that your feet are what your entire body balances upon. Once your body becomes bigger, and especially when you become very round in the middle, your feet must grow to compensate. You wouldn't want to tip over, would you?

A baby is God's opinion that the world should go on.

-- Carl Sandburg

NOTES:

_____

_____

_____

_____

_____

_____

THINGS TO ASK YOUR DOCTOR:

_____

_____

_____

_____

_____

_____

_____

CHAPTER 13

HAIR COLOR AND TEXTURE

If you're hoping your long, straight as a board, blonde hair will remain the same after childbirth, think again. Most moms report that their hair changed drastically after having a baby. My straight blonde hair developed waves and started getting much darker. I think it would be brown if I didn't maintain my trips to the salon for highlights.

I've talked to some women who report straight hair getting very curly and others who say their curly hair went completely straight. Your hair texture can also change from silky smooth to coarse and dull. Some women report drastic changes in their hair color, such as brunettes turning red. Every story is unique. What will YOU look like after your child is born?

Hair is somewhat a reflection on diet. Having a baby takes a lot of nutrients out of a woman's body. Therefore, in order to have the most healthy looking hair, one should have the proper diet and nutritional supplements.

Another thing about hair and new moms, and this goes for moms of every age: Don't do something drastic with your hair as soon as you have a baby. This is the worst pitfall for some new moms. You think you want something easy, so you run out and get a perm. The result is that you end up looking like a poodle and hate every picture you have taken with your baby. You start out with long hair and chop it all off so it doesn't get in your way.

Now your husband doesn't recognize you and you look like a little boy. Resist the urge to dramatically alter your appearance. Rather, continue to see your same hair stylist and ask for a slightly different and easier to manage hair style that will allow you to enter motherhood with grace and dignity.

A new baby is like the beginning of all things-wonder, hope, a dream of possibilities.
-- Eda J. Le Shan

A baby is sunshine and moonbeams and more brightening your world as never before.
-- Author Unknown

NOTES:

_____

_____

_____

_____

_____

_____

THINGS TO ASK YOUR DOCTOR:

_____

_____

_____

_____

_____

_____

CHAPTER 14

SEXUAL DESIRE

Once you could have sex anywhere and anytime you wanted. Now, you almost have to schedule it. That does take some of the romance out of it, but hey, it's that or nothing. Some nights it goes kind of like this: "Are you kidding me? I haven't had a good night's sleep since I can't remember when and you want to get playful?" This is probably the most difficult part. "Just think how good you will sleep afterwards," he says jokingly. What he means is how good HE will sleep afterwards. If possible, try to have sex on the nights when it's his turn to get up with the baby. That way you really can enjoy a good night's sleep.

Here's what you need to do. First, make sure you have a good baby monitor. This way you can hear your baby crying with your bedroom door closed (and locked if you have an older child who can walk). Monitors only work one direction, they transmit sound from the unit you place in the baby's room to the speaker you have in your room. Sound does not travel back to the baby. This is why you close your door – so you can enjoy your time with your husband and not worry about waking the baby.

Second, get used to and comfortable with your new body. This is probably the next hardest part. When your stomach stretches out at its full term limit, there is a lot of skin that just doesn't disappear. As we age our skin loses some of its

73

elasticity. You may have extra skin that just won't go away. Your breasts used to be perky and now they are pointing toward the floor. You must learn to love your body all over again. Your husband still loves you and finds you attractive. Look at him. Has he put on a few pounds since you married him? Don't you still think he's sexy? Of course you do! Our bodies change over time and so we must adjust our thoughts.

Now that you're feeling like a sex kitten again, buy some new lingerie and keep it for those special times when you really want to drive your man crazy. Surprise him. He'll love it.

Babies are a link between angels and man.

-- Author Unknown

NOTES:

_____

_____

_____

_____

_____

_____

THINGS TO ASK YOUR DOCTOR:

_____

_____

_____

_____

_____

_____

_____

CHAPTER 15

IMMUNITY

Ever wonder why business women with small children are always sick? Well, it's not just because of their little Petri dishes (ahem, I mean children). Yes, children do bring home all sorts of germs once they begin attending a formal daycare or even going to school. The little ones need to build up their resistance to different germs, bacteria, viruses, etc., so it is a good thing to have them exposed to germs. Parents have usually built up their own immune system and should be able to ward off catching things from their little children.

However, unless you're one of the lucky ones that have a child who sleeps through the night, *every night*, then be prepared to get sick right along with them. Sleep isn't only important to regulate your metabolism; it's also important in keeping your immune system up to par. Research has shown that our bodies do a lot of work while we think we are asleep. It's a wonder you can wake up feeling so refreshed in the morning when your body has been so busy during the night building up its army of defenses.

People who do not get enough sleep are the first ones to get sick. Have you ever noticed how your body tells you that an illness is on its way? The first sign is that you feel completely worn out. Exhausted! This is your body's way of telling you to get some sleep so it can do its work. If you listen to your body and have the ability (and by ability I mean someone else to do the cooking, cleaning,

77

taking care of the baby, feeding the dog, etc.) to go right to bed and get some sleep, most of the time you can avoid getting sick.

On the other hand, if you push yourself and keep on going at the same intensity level that you normally do, don't be surprised if you feel like you were hit by a truck within the next 24 to 48 hours. This is when you have no choice. You must cease all activity and get some rest. If you can't find someone to help around the house, then you can expect to be sick for awhile.

Babies are always more trouble than you thought - and more wonderful.

-- Charles Osgood

NOTES:

_____

_____

_____

_____

_____

_____

THINGS TO ASK YOUR DOCTOR:

_____

_____

_____

_____

_____

_____

_____

CHAPTER 16

LOSS OF PERSONAL TIME

If you have a baby when you're in your 20's you are probably not set in your ways yet. You've just recently moved out of your parents' house and adding a baby to your mix just means that you are now the parent and your parents are the grandparents.

It's quite different when you are in your 40's and have gotten used to doing things your way. Simple things are no longer simple. Hey, there's a great new movie coming out this weekend. It's the third in the trilogy and you've been waiting anxiously for it to hit the theaters. It's way too loud to take the baby, she'll cry. You must find a babysitter. Your parents are out of town, your friends are going to the movie, and your siblings have plans. Everyone has plans. How can that be? You miss the premiere. Everyone is talking about it at work the next day. It was awesome! Amazing! Best of the three, they say. You vow to go see it this weekend, provided you can find a babysitter, and can stay awake.

Maybe you are like me and enjoy spending lazy Saturday mornings tending to your garden. You enjoy picking roses to have fresh flowers in the house, transplanting things that have outgrown their pots, checking out the vegetable garden to see what's ripe this weekend. Now you look outside through blurry eyes and notice that there are no roses, there is a jungle out there and nobody has tended to it in months. You wish you could take care of it because you enjoy the beauty that your garden brings to your yard, but the baby needs you and you can't justify spending time doing something you enjoy when you have the responsibility to take care of your baby.

It's summer now and you have a nice swimming pool. The raft is floating on the water and there is a gentle breeze. Wouldn't it feel nice to put on your swimsuit and just float around on the raft for awhile and enjoy the sun, the breeze and the sounds of sparrows chirping nearby? First of all, you no longer look good in that bikini. It's time to invest in a one-piece swim suit. Second, you know that once you get all comfy on that raft, the baby will wake up from her all too short nap and need your attention. You would take a nap yourself but you know better. The moment you fall asleep is the baby's queue to wake up. So you just sit inside and watch her sleep, dreaming of the day you can get back on the raft in the pool.

If I could give you one gift, I would give you the ability to see yourself as I see you, so you could see how truly special you are.

-- Author Unknown

NOTES:

_____

_____

_____

_____

_____

_____

THINGS TO ASK YOUR DOCTOR:

_____

_____

_____

_____

_____

_____

_____

CHAPTER 17
A TYPICAL WORKDAY

Let's take a look at a typical day. For years you've gone to bed when you wanted and arose in plenty of time to get ready for work. You put on your nice dress or suit and stop by the local coffee shop and head to work. Simple. Here's how that can change.

You go to bed only to be awoken countless times during the night for one reason or another and finally get into a really good REM sleep pattern around 5 am. By 5:10 the baby wakes up and will absolutely not go back to sleep. No amount of bribery works. You're up. You feel like a zombie. You think that you may have gotten about 4 or 5 hours of sleep here and there. Feed the baby, change the baby's diaper, dress the baby, find somewhere to put the baby so she doesn't hurt herself while you take a shower.

All set, baby is safe in her crib and you hop in the shower. Just as you get shampoo in your hair, you hear her crying or is it screaming? Barely clean and rinsed off, you get out of the shower to see what's wrong with the baby. Nothing. She just wanted to see you. You're awake now from the adrenaline rush of thinking your baby was hurt, but that quickly dissipates. You get dressed for work, pack a diaper bag, grab some formula for the baby and start to head out. Wait, you forgot your purse. Need that. Pack up the car and buckle in the baby. Time to hit the road. You're hungry aren't you?

You're thinking that you should have grabbed some breakfast while you were still at home.

You decide to swing by the coffee shop. You pull into the parking lot and unbuckle the baby and carry her into the coffee shop with you. Ask for a muffin and a coffee and now you're wondering how you're going to carry all of that. You have a baby, your purse, coffee, a muffin and you have to get your car keys out to unlock the car door. You manage, but you would swear it's 100 degrees outside now because sweat is pouring off your forehead.

You arrive at the baby sitter's house to drop off the baby for the day. You carry in the car seat with your baby still buckled in, the diaper bag and your purse. You feel like you've been to the gym. You are panting and sweating again. You get back into your car and let out a big sigh. Now all you have to do is get yourself to work. You arrive, only 10 minutes late this time, and realize that you forgot your jewelry. Those earrings and matching necklace that look so good with your outfit are still at home. A couple of hours later when you walk past the mirror in the restroom, you notice that you forgot to put on your lipstick. You wonder why nobody told you.

When you get off work you can't wait to see your little bundle of joy. You hurry to the sitter to pick her up. She smiles when she sees you, your heart melts. How sweet. Just then, you remember that you're out of diapers at home and you must stop at the store on your way home. You grab the car seat, diaper bag and baby and pack up the car. Get to the grocery store and unpack the car. Your baby is too little to sit in the shopping cart, so you balance the car seat on the basket and try to see over it while you are pushing it through the store.

You finish shopping and are ready to go back to the car. It's raining. You don't have an umbrella. You think to yourself "this is going to be fun." You put the baby in the car first, of course. Then you unload the groceries and finally get yourself in the car. Soaking wet . . . again. At least this time it's not from your own perspiration.

Home at last. Unpack the car, change the baby's diaper, put her somewhere nearby so she can watch you cook dinner. About half way through cooking dinner your husband arrives at home and says "I've had the most hectic day." You laugh. You have to. It's either that or cry.

All you can think of is bedtime. You are exhausted! You have been going strong all day since the very moment you, as a zombie, crawled out of bed. Feeling much the same way at 8:00 p.m., you collapse. You almost instantly fall asleep. It's

9:30 and you hear the baby crying. She's hungry. You get up and feed her and are back in bed by 9:50. Your mind starts wandering. Finally at 10:45, you're almost asleep and you are dreaming of a baby crying. Wait. That's not a dream. That's your baby. She's wet and needs a diaper change. Out of bed again, you stumble to baby to change her diaper. Poop! Ahh, why didn't you think to bring the wipes with you this time? Where are they again? Need to turn on a light. Oh that's just great, now baby is wide awake and wants to play.

She's finally asleep and it's after midnight. Sleep, precious sleep where are you? There's that crying again. What time is it? 2:00 a.m. Did you fall asleep? It doesn't really seem like it, but then it also doesn't seem like you've been in bed all that long. Who knows? "I'm coming!!" Sheesh, don't babies know that they've woken you up and you'll

90

get there just as soon as you can get your feet on the floor and focus your vision?

Hungry again? Are you serious? Okay fine, just please stop crying, I'm working on it. The clock reads 2:35 as you get back in bed. Exhausted. You fall into a deep sleep. It's 5:10 (already) and the sun is not even up, but your baby is. Tuesday. Oh my gosh, is it really only Tuesday? Sigh. Here we go again.

I had a really nice arrangement with my husband. We would take turns for the night time wake up calls. He'd take one night and then I'd take the next night. It's really the only way to do it. This way, at least one of you can stay in bed and try to get some sleep. You may still wake up when the baby cries, but if you don't have to physically get out of bed, it's a lot easier to fall back asleep. You might even try ear plugs when it's not your night to get up.

When you look at your life, the greatest happinesses are family happinesses.

-- Joyce Brothers

You don't choose your family. They are God's gift to you, as you are to them.

-- Desmond Tutu

NOTES:

_____

_____

_____

_____

_____

THINGS TO ASK YOUR DOCTOR:

_____

_____

_____

_____

_____

_____

_____

CHAPTER 18

DAYCARE

So you grew up, went to college and moved far away from your parents and family for the perfect career. Then you decide to start a family once your career has been established. Get ready to watch your paycheck slip away from you. Whether you choose a nanny or a formal daycare, the cost is astonishing. In Southern California, you can expect to spend anywhere from $200 to $500 per week for your infant child. This cost does not include diapers, wipes or formula. So, you may want to have a little nest egg before you get pregnant. Daycare the first year will cost you between $10,000 and $20,000 for one child. Fortunately, the cost does go down as your bundle of joy gets older.

I had a toddler and a 5-year old in a formal daycare at the same time. The toddler was $325 a week and the 5-year old was $210 a week. That's roughly $2300 per month, or $27,600 per year. The tuition is not based on income, everyone pays the same whether you're making minimum wage or you earn a six-figure income. Now you see why my shoes are black and all my clothes go with black shoes. I just recently did some math and realized that by the time both children are in first grade, I will have spent close to $100,000 on daycare. Wow! In some states, you can buy a nice home for that kind of money.

Now you may be considering the idea of a nanny. Certainly you could get someone to come to your home and watch your children, do some laundry and light cleaning for that much money. You might even be fortunate enough to have someone who speaks another language and then your children would have the advantage of being bilingual before they ever even start formal school. A great deal of research must be done in advance in order to get what's right for you and your family. There are many placement agencies that you can find on the internet, or by asking friends who have children.

I had no idea child care would be so expensive. Even after my oldest child started first grade, I still had to pay for before and after school care, which seemed cheap at only $326 a month. But then I'm also paying for lunches and school supplies. Oh, and during the summer, the cost goes up to $140 a week, so it's almost double what it is during the school year.

You may think that you can get ahead by claiming child care as a deduction on your taxes. You can claim it, but only up to a certain amount and, trust me, it's nowhere near what you actually pay. Some companies offer a flexible spending account for child care whereby you can have up to $5000 deducted from your paycheck pre-tax and then get reimbursed upon showing documentation of expenses being paid. I blow through that $5,000 before the year is half way gone. The rest is just money in and money out with no tax advantages.

You might be like me, an only child who loves to buy things for ME, and then you get pregnant and you're buying things for mini-me. This too is okay because you will find much greater joy in buying tiny little clothes for your baby than you ever will buying clothes two sizes larger for yourself. Forget corporate America for now, just enjoy the tiny person that you have just created and spend quality time bonding with him or her.

You are worried about seeing him spend his early years in doing nothing. What! Is it nothing to be happy? Nothing to skip, play, and run around all day long? Never in his life will he be so busy again.

~Jean-Jacques Rousseau, *Emile*, 1762

A three year old child is a being who gets almost as much fun out of a fifty-six dollar set of swings as it does out of finding a small green worm.

~Bill Vaughan

NOTES:

_____

_____

_____

_____

_____

_____

THINGS TO ASK YOUR DOCTOR:

_____

_____

_____

_____

_____

_____

_____

CHAPTER 19

POTTY TRAINING

I'm still trying to figure out this one! My husband's grandmother had eight children. She loves teasing me and telling me how they were all potty trained by the time they were one year old and never did one of them wet the bed. I sometimes wonder if she's a super hero, just got lucky, or has no true recollection of what happened over 40 years ago. Just kidding grandma! I honestly think it has more to do with cloth versus disposable diapers than with how you attempt to train your child.

When babies are wearing cloth diapers and they urinate, they feel wet. They are uncomfortable, and they immediately let you know that they want their diaper changed. With disposable diapers, babies rarely ever "feel" wet. The diapers are so good at keeping the wetness away from the baby's tender tushie that the baby never knows that they are wet. The "I am wet" signal that goes to the brain doesn't work unless the disposable diaper becomes totally saturated, whereas with a cloth diaper, the signal transmits immediately, the first time the baby pees or poops in the diaper. I'll bet if you ask around, you'll find that moms who used cloth diapers had their children potty trained much easier than those who had their babies in disposable diapers.

Of course, I was using disposable diapers because that was the "in" thing to do at the time. Of course, now that we have gone "green" more and more people are going back to cloth diapers in an attempt to save the environment. I wish I had used cloth diapers! I was told that girls are easier to potty train than boys. My first child was a girl, so I started trying to train her at 18 months. I bought the cute little port-a-potty for her, stenciled her name on it and figured it would be a breeze. Not so much. By the time she turned three, I had watched the potty training videos with her so many times that I truly hated the song that they sing in the videos. She would wear pull ups, but instead of using the toilet, she would hide in the curtains when she would "concentrate" to get the job done.

Finally, one day a miracle occurred when we forgot to put a pull up on her when she took a nap – she awoke completely dry. Yay! We enjoyed about a year of this until the second child was born. The oldest, who was then four, started having trouble staying dry at night. We had to buy pull ups again.

We tried a number of solutions, none of which really worked. We tried putting an alarm clock in her room to wake her up twice during the night so she'd get up and use the restroom. For a little while that worked, but then she started sleeping thru the alarm and it was waking up everyone else in the house except her. We would have to get out of bed, go to her room, turn off the alarm and tell her to wake up and go to the bathroom. But then we noticed that the alarm was waking up the baby too, who was not as inclined to go right back to sleep.

Of course, we tried the obvious thing and limited her liquid consumption before going to bed and having her use the restroom immediately before going to bed, but that didn't seem to work either. I think what happened is a double-whammy for her. First of all, she had the sibling rivalry thing going on. The baby was now getting the attention she was used to getting and so she reverted to doing things that babies do – because that gets her attention. Secondly, when she started first grade, she was no longer taking naps. By the time she went to bed at night, she was so completely exhausted that she could literally sleep thru almost anything (including the blaring alarm clock right next to her bed). She has even slept thru earthquakes. Yes, we live in California.

The second child is supposed to be easier to potty train because they see their older sibling doing something and they want to be just like him/her. Ever hear the phrase monkey-see-monkey-do? I cannot believe how true it really is with children. Pray that your first child is a good one! My second child started wanting to use the potty around the age of two, but I discovered that all she really wanted to do was use the toilet paper. What is it with kids and disposable items? She would unroll an entire roll of toilet paper just because it was fun, but she wouldn't just unroll it and leave it there, she'd keep tearing it off at intervals and wadding it up and either throwing it in the trash can or in the toilet. Yes, we had to use a plunger more than once for this action.

When my youngest was just over three years old, she starting using the potty like a big girl. I tried really hard with the first child to get her potty trained so she could attend preschool (lots of one-on-one time, pretty panties, praise, etc.), but then I found out that children will potty train themselves on their own time table. When they're ready mentally and emotionally, they will let you know.

Some kids prefer to wear pull-ups during the daytime so they could continue playing and not have to stop to use the restroom. Beware of anything that interrupts play time!

When dealing with night time accidents, I decided that rather than negative reinforcement (making the child feel bad for wetting at night), I'd opt for positive reinforcement in monetary form – hey whatever works. "Hey girls, if you wake up and you're dry, I'll give you a dollar!" Funny how quickly they started waking up at night when money was on the line. Oh yeah, there's another expense I failed to mention earlier. It seems as if bribery works very well with the little ones.

Children's talent to endure stems from their ignorance of alternatives.

~Maya Angelou
I Know Why the Caged Bird Sings, **1969**

NOTES:

_____

_____

_____

_____

_____

_____

THINGS TO ASK YOUR DOCTOR:

_____

_____

_____

_____

_____

_____

_____

CHAPTER 20

WHO AM I NOW?
LOSS OF IDENTITY

It's funny that when you get married you're excited about your new last name . . . the new you. You practice writing your new name over and over again because you want your signature to look just perfect. But before you know it, people are referring to you as so-and-so's mom. You no longer have a real name. I became "Jackie's mom" just 16 months after I was married. Going to work is the only place people refer to me by my real name.

Even after I had my second child, I'm still called "Jackie's mom" by the daycare that I use for Katie. They all know me as Jackie's mom and wouldn't know it was me if they read my name in the obituary column of the newspaper unless the story read "Jackie's mom is survived by . . . ."

Something else that happens with the weight gain is that I don't even look like me anymore when I look in the mirror. All of a sudden, I have turned into my mom! (Not that there's anything wrong with that.) There must be something about responsibility and being serious that takes away that youthful spirit. I saw many of my friends go through this change in their late 20's or early 30's, but not me. I had no children and was footloose and fancy free. I could still fit into my high school cheerleading dress at 35, men still honked and whistled at me as I was walking down the street. I had all the energy of an 18 year old. Life was good.

109

Don't get me wrong, life is still good . . . it's just different. The "me" that I knew so well after 39 years vanished. Most of my friends are different now than they were a few years ago. I don't get to go out to the clubs or see new movies on opening night. The people that I used to do that with still do that, they just do it with other friends that either have no children, or who have children that have already grown up and moved out.

What's more confusing is that I don't even want to do most of those things anymore. All I want is to get a good night's sleep, and that means for the kids to sleep through the night and past 7:00 a.m. Most people with little kids don't even stay up to watch the ball drop in Times Square on New Year's Eve. That would mean going to bed after midnight and waking up a few hours later to feed and/or change the baby. After that you have to try to make up all those lost hours of sleep, which is nearly impossible. I figure the New Year will arrive whether I'm asleep or awake and I'll just watch it on the news the next day.

The Tournament of Roses Parade is on January 1 (most years). I never knew that it started at 8:00 a.m. I always thought the parade started "early" in the morning because I always missed the beginning of it and had to watch one of the encore showings to see the entire parade. These days I have been up for at least two hours, have had coffee, breakfast, a shower and wonder why it's taking so long for the parade to start. I even asked my husband if they changed the start time of the parade because now it seems to start so late in the morning.

Anyone who thinks the art of conversation is dead ought to tell a child to go to bed.

~Robert Gallagher

NOTES:

_____

_____

_____

_____

_____

_____

_____

THINGS TO ASK YOUR DOCTOR:

_____

_____

_____

_____

_____

_____

_____

CHAPTER 21
DON'T BE SURPRISED IF . . .

Don't be surprised if you don't get stretch marks. When you get older, your skin loses some of its elasticity. The only good thing about that is not getting stretch marks. I was quite worried that I would get stretch marks. I thought everyone did. I was very happy that I didn't get a single one! There is no guarantee, but I think you are a lot less likely to get stretch marks if you get pregnant for the first time after the age of 35.

Another thing that surprised me was that my ribcage expanded. This may only happen if you are short-waisted, but don't be surprised if your "core" gets larger after having children. My first child had her foot in my ribs for quite awhile. I can definitely see that my ribs stick out more now than they used to.

Don't be surprised if all of a sudden you can't remember things. I don't know how it's possible, but it seems as if being pregnant and having children destroys brain cells. My short term memory is all but gone. Things I used to be able to remember easily have somehow flown out the window.

Here's an example. My boss's wife calls and he's on the other line. She says "have him call me." I agree and then hang up and continue doing my work. I completely forget that she called . . . until she calls again. "Is he still on the phone?" Oh no!

Having children is both good and bad for your memory. The bad part is the forgetting, the good part is having someone to remember for you. You can always tell your kids "remind me to buy bread at the store" and most of the time they actually do remind me. Of course, they are kids so sometimes I get the "don't forget to buy bread mom" when I'm putting them to bed at night or when I'm getting dressed for work.

Probably the worst part of memory loss is when talking with your children while not really paying attention. I just cringe when my daughter starts out a sentence with "Remember mommy, you said I could have . . ."

Children seldom misquote. In fact, they usually repeat word for word what you shouldn't have said.

~Author Unknown

115

NOTES:

_____

_____

_____

_____

_____

_____

THINGS TO ASK YOUR DOCTOR:

_____

_____

_____

_____

_____

_____

_____

CONCLUSION

I hope you have found this book useful and informative and have enjoyed a laugh or two along the way. Sometimes you must laugh in order to keep from crying. Having children is a blessing and you will learn that you can do much more than you ever thought possible. You will also find that you are much stronger than you thought. You will carry a 20 pound child in one arm while toting a diaper bag and your purse with the other.

You will learn how to cook with one hand tied behind your back – or actually with one arm holding your baby, but it will seem the same. You will be able to multitask even if you never knew what that word meant before. You will be able to feed your baby, talk on the phone, answer an email, and tell the dog to stop chewing on the baby's toys all at the same time. You will be a superhero to your child. You are the one he or she comes to whenever they are hurt or just need the reassurance that they are loved and everything will be alright.

You will be more than a woman, you will be a mommy! You are the only one in the world that will have the mother/child bond that is so precious. I never understood how it could be possible to love someone so much that you would die for them, until I became a mom. I now know the sacrifices my mom made for me and I appreciate her a whole lot more. There's something about being a mom that cannot be taught or learned until you actually are a mom. Instinct kicks in and you will have all the tools you need to care for and protect your precious gift from God.

Remember, hugs and kisses can fix almost everything . . . and if those don't work, there's always duct tape!

INFORMATIONAL LINKS

I have provided these links to you should you wish to find more information on your pregnancy, health, or children. Some of the statistics and other information contained in the previous chapters were found by starting at these links.

For a guide to what happens week by week, the following websites have great information:

www.babycenter.com

http://www.pregnancy.com/

http://www.pregnancyguideonline.com/

For information on cord blood:

http://www.cordblood.com/?fbid=drU7HyW8V7O

For a complete medical perspective on miscarriage, the Mayo Clinic has a great article at:

http://www.mayoclinic.com/health/miscarriage/DS01
105

For information on protein meal replacement shakes (for weight loss):

http://www.dena.bodybyvi.com/

For information on Vi-Pak nutritional supplements and how to qualify for a free BMW:

http://www.dena.myvi.net

For all around good information, I also like:

http://www.doctoroz.com/

http://babyplaceonline.com/

http://www.justmommies.com/babychannel.shtml

Made in the USA
Middletown, DE
07 March 2024